G000037712

Laura Taylor was born into a working-class family in the North of England in 1968. She has challenged arbitrary forms of authority all her life. Obsessed by words and language since childhood, everything fell into place when she stumbled across semiotics and its psychedelic tentacles.

SPEAKING in TONGUES
Laura Taylor

Flapjack Press
flapjackpress.co.uk

Exploring the synergy between performance and the page

Published in 2021 by Flapjack Press
Salford, Gtr Manchester
⊕ flapjackpress.co.uk
f Flapjack Press 🐦 FlapjackPress
▶ Flapjack Press

ISBN 978-1-8381185-9-4

Cover photo by Neil McCartney

Printed by Imprint Digital
Exeter, Devon
⊕ digital.imprint.co.uk

FSC

MAN
CHE
STER
A UNESCO City
of Literature

To my precious daughter Alex,
for everything we've been through,
and for my darling Bob Kettle, love of my life.

And to all my absent friends too soon gone
– Shirl, Graham, Boo, Bex and Jinks –
thanks for the love, laughs, and forever-held memories.

Contents

"Now, brothers and sisters, if I come to you and speak in tongues, what good will I be to you, unless I bring you some revelation or knowledge or prophecy or word of instruction?"
1 Corinthians, 14:6

"Language is never innocent."
Roland Barthes, *Writing Degree Zero*

"Words are like a certain person
Who can't say what they mean
Don't mean what they say"
Tom Tom Club, 'Wordy Rappinghood'

I started putting this collection together just as my second book, *Fault Lines*, was being published in 2018. I already had the title and a handful of poems that were just right for it.

Then in January 2020, Covid-19 began its deadly creep across the globe and our worlds were changed forever.

We have lived through a time of national trauma, barely protected by a Tory government which has failed us at almost every turn. In many cases, they made a bad situation much worse through a combination of greed, incompetence, mixed messaging and catastrophic decision-making. In an interesting twist, they were also forced to adopt socialistic policies in order that the economy didn't just disappear down the toilet.

It was impossible not to write about. The slippery and inconclusive condition of language could be seen and heard in the use of mixed messaging – lending itself particularly well to the concept of speaking in tongues. So, what began as one book morphed into this, with a hefty middle section devoted to a 'World-Beating Corona Suite'.

It looks like we're coming out of it now, albeit with the threat of other deadly mutations doing the rounds. I hope that when you read this, you are regaining some optimism and a sense of orientation. I dearly hope to see you in a field some day soon, by a fire, where we'll chat shit, sing, pass the rum, have a hug, dance beneath the stars and try not to scratch our scars until they weep.

Until then, take care and stay safe.

x

Laura Taylor

Origin

This began with whispered words,
bites from shiny apples,
a desire
to command, create;
a hunger to articulate intensity,
to mechanise a melody inside.

This commenced with prephonation;
tutoring of simple lips,
tentatively glossolalic.
Patterns forming,
disconnected information circling itself,
pulling at phonetic cords of morphemes

and spitting out bubbles just for fun, in between.

I did not suck my thumb.
I used hydraulic energy
and learned to work the motors of the muscles
in my head; masticating syllables,
exorcising scribbles made of air and formless urges;
engineering frenulous activity

and spitting out bubbles just for fun, in between.

This began and will not end until the breath begins to fade,
'til incantation drains away and starts to dig itself a grave,
knowing that it's naked and emaciating daily;
'til my tongue begins to wilt,
and the bricks I used to build myself
a living wall of symbols
fall apart, decay and die,
and disappear.

Until I do not spit out bubbles just for fun, anymore.

Speaking in Tongues

They said
Too clever
for your own good.

I heard
that it was not for me,
like olives and halloumi

and
Must you question everything?
Unintended irony.

They own
the land and property.

I face
reduced mortality.

The *politics of envy*
are for the likes of me.

The politics of greed
are what I clearly see.

I learned
that thought-provoking words should not be used in school,
like primogeniture, or cultural hegemony.

They said
What do you want to be?
A nurse or secretary?

Then
Tell me what the poem means.

I said
that it was not for me.
Refused, would not reduce.

There is one meaning, learn it well
so you can pass your O-level.

I didn't.

Instead
I tore my tongue in two,
threw salt across a wall of eyes,
soaked my throat in dissonance,
and didn't
listen to their lies.
I saw that all the world's for me,
that they could keep dishonesty,
and I laughed,
eating olives and halloumi.

From her hollow hauls a thread,
an ache of indigo,
ten tongues long and a lifetime ago
and it's not my grief,
but I recognize the weave
and the shadow on her whispered tapestry.

Silk-embroidered sky and sea
salt heritage and history.
Untangling a violet braid,
she thumbs it smooth repeatedly;
it wasn't greed that made her run
from home and hunger's bite.

Bullets bearing tiny names
take flight across her teeth.
She never smiles.
The ocean's echo in her throat
goes on for miles
of time and space.

There are no rainbows on her breath,
no golden light between her sighs.
There's only ache,
deep-dyed in indigo
and double-hemmed
to make it safe.

The woods are alcoholic.
It's a well-known fact.
They must think I'm daft,
but I wasn't born yesterday.
I can see it with my own eyes.
Diamond Whites litter paths,
crumpled up and cast aside
carelessly. They disgust me.
No one in their right minds
would come in here at night.

The copse has got a problem.
There's clearly an addiction
to weather-based oblivion –
White Storm, Frosty Jacks, Lightning.
8% pleasure, 99p
of urination and a 3 litre stream
of my righteous castigation.
Don't give the trees money,
they will spend it all on booze.
Always do.

Look at where it's set itself on fire!
Must be so blind drunk it doesn't care
that it's burned itself alive.
Some can't see the woods for the trees,
but not me.
I bet they're foreign too.
Coming over here, ruining our common ground
while hard-working woodland
is cleared for affordable housing.
Makes me sick it does.

I'm not as stupid as I look.
I can see its tent tucked behind a bush,
no doubt to hide its grubby stash.
Doesn't even bother
to put its filthy sleeping bag away,
just leaves it there, spewing
from the zipper,
getting ranker
and more putrid
by the day.

Plump

In hush of dusk, a brown-backed flush
of silent migrants gather.
No passport checks, no border guards.
They wait, prepare to feather air
to Beauly Firth, to fertile ground, to safety
in formation.

We stop to watch the tea-time mob,
pass comment on the novelty.
Remember they were brought to grace
a private space of regal greed,
ornaments against their will,
and now considered pests
to be controlled.

Fickle England pricks the eggs
of babies loathed before they're born.
Their problem is they made themselves
too comfortably at home;
it doesn't matter where they roam,
they'll always be pariahs,
never celebrated travellers
on pedestals.

A chorus of chaotic honks signals their departure.
We watch them breaking through the trees,
a genius of vortices, untrammelled
and behove to no authority.
Unravelling in bright-eyed glee,
we laugh in solidarity;
the Earth's a common treasury for all.

I'm Not a Racist, but

I haven't got the guts
to own my own discrimination.
Islam's not a race
and I think I'm being clever
but I'll leather you in seconds
for being a different colour to my own
funny tone. I'm actually not white,
more mottled pink and purple,
a sort of meaty shade,
but you're gonna be in trouble
if you say so, as a joke.

I just don't have the guts
to own my own beliefs.
I get defensive, in denial
of my xenophobic deeds,
as if my ears cannot hear
the sounds in my mouth,
as if my fists cannot feel
the nose, broke and brown.
I'm not a coward. Far from it.
I'll punch and kick and kill,
spill my animosity
like beer upon the table
but there's no way I'm a racist, mate.

Yeh, I like to lob bananas
on the pitches that I paid for,
make monkey sounds,
throw pennies, but
it's just for shits 'n' giggles!
Take it easy! It's a joke!

Everyone's offended!
And nowadays,
if you say you're English…
people laugh.
Stewart fucking Lee.

I wrap my sunburned back
in an imperial rag, fail to recognise
the deeply hypocritical stance
of The Empire.
Going over there, taking their lives.
I haven't got the bollocks
to own my own bias.
I'm all wind and piss
plus a full English breakfast
in an ex-pat's pub based in Benidorm.
I don't bother with the lingo,
everyone speaks English.

And I'm not a racist, but
it really gets my goat
when they speak in funny languages.
So ignorant!
I think illegal immigrants
get benefits and houses,
and I don't even think about
the meaning of 'illegal'
when I'm foaming at the mouth
and spewing bile about
their trainers being Nike.
How can they afford them?

I never say 'Chinese'
when I order from the takeaway,
or 'stani' 'cause it takes too long,
2 syllables too many.

Take it easy! It's a joke!
Stop being so offended!
And I'm not being funny but
I am.
My best mate is black,
blind, gay, dead, a lie
to try and justify
my bigotry.

And for fuck's sake, you can't say
Happy Christmas any more
or blackboard, Baa Baa
Black Sheep, gollywog
or White Lives Matter!!!
It's Political Correctness gone mad!!!!!!!!
I use exclamation marks
more than the average man
and I demand free speech
as a white human being.
It's my right!
God given!

Like I say I'm not a racist, but
I am a gutless hate machine,
reject until I'm apoplectic
every single slur
against my character.
I just think we're superior, is all!
White is Might,
Blood and Honour,
string 'em up.
Wotcha mean,
we come from Africa?!

I'm not a racist, but…

Take two over-ripe ovaries,
one weathered womb,
five consecutive nights of broken sleep
and enough perspiration to make a brand new ocean.
Congratulations – you are now a topographical feature
(or a gatefold concept prog-rock album).
Perhaps you could call that ocean *The Sea of WhatTheActualFuck*,
or for a more formal, though wildly optimistic, nomenclature:
The Sea of Opportunities.

Add *The Sea of Opportunities* to five loads of bedding
and mix well with an exhausted yawn.
Quickly add one ounce of oestrogen
then remove from mixture.
Add another ounce of oestrogen
then extract double that amount.
You are now entering the *Emotional Rollercoaster Zone*.
Please do not fly off the handle or someone may get hurt.
Stew six pounds of self-esteem and set aside.
Pre-heat oven to *Gas Mark Chernobyl*.
Begin to wonder if it's hot in here or if it's just you…
tear off top with all the elegance of a rampaging baby elephant.

Reapply apparel.
Dredge the flour of confusion over everyday tasks
and stare into middle distance.
Bring pan of baseless resentment to the boil
and simmer for one whole day.
If this process is disturbed, slam the door (repeatedly)
and sob one gallon of hot salt fury.
Check oven.

Is it hot in here?
Rip off frock in one demented dress-killing action.

Reapply attire.
If, at this stage, the mixture seems a little dry
and mortified, try not to cry.
Add water-based moisture.
Look for the self-esteem you set aside earlier.
Keep looking.
It must be *somewhere* for God's sake!
Check that bloody oven.
Wrestle aggressively with aggravating garb.
Open every single window. And door.
Ignore the cries of the weak.
They can put a bloody jumper on if they're *that* cold.

Consider giving up clothing once and for all.
Discard recipe.
Throw black cohosh, soy, red clover, sage, wild yam
and St John's Wort into the bin
and kick it hard to the corner for good measure.
Ring GP for HRT.

Delia can fuck off.

Login*

You're not supposed to write it down,
but I do because it's you within
the market stalls, summoning aromas, bars,
brawls, and all the girls you bought
you said were called Rose.

A salty dog legacy; inherited protection.
It's logged within your history,
existed well before me, the internet,
or Civvy Street.
Now it lives in echoes
in a box beneath the bed,
catching dust instead of breath.

Even 'til the end, you were 21 again,
telling and retelling, embellishing
unconsciously: truth became fable,
myth; became passwords,
indelible. Inked in the mark of a man
with his tongue ever relishing the taste
of his salad days
$ingapore1966*

*Your password must contain at least one special character.

From packet and clipper,
from Royal destroyer,
with prayer and with hymn
and a rum-drenched Amen,
goodbye to the matelot and captain;
so long to the boatswain and master.
We're chanting to ease up the passing.

The last one is sung in a million tongues.
Grief-soaked and lonesome
haul hard on the Solent.
The last one is sung by them all.

A plash of committal.
The lash of the wind
on castanet skeletons;
fishes who swim
with the daddies and grandads
o'er Horse and Dean Sand
to the fort there at Spitbank,
in caskets so grand.
We're chanting to ease up the passing.

The last one is sung in a million tongues,
salty and free,
in full liberty.
The last one is sung by them all.

You riggers and stokers
set sail to drop anchor
where lads can relax,

and rations are massive
and backs never lashed,
nor words spoke in anger.
We're chanting to ease up the passing.

The last one is sung in a million tongues,
no work to be done,
no work to be done.
The last one is sung by them all.

They roll and they pitch
and they whistle and drift;
white horses to roam
and ride them to home,
to sleep in the ocean and sing everlasting.
We're chanting to ease up the passing.

The last one is sung by a million tongues.
We'll lie here forever
and rock in the weather.
The last one is sung by them all.

Molecular emancipation is not a life goal

though I hold it close, don't share
because it never seems to comfort.
That suction, the speed of it,
complete loss of structure
and all responsibility.

Imagine being so free.
Consider being cloud, becoming sky,
wind-roused, making rain
for stranger's eyes,
radiating shine
in a parallel shaft of shadow particles.
Maybe on your wavelength.
Maybe not.

A God's ray spied by a girl aged nine
in Fukushima, holding hands with her brother
on a Sunday.
To actually *be*
aurora borealis, noumena;
unknowable, invisible to man.

Like I say, it's not a goal,
but transmutation to divinity is kind of reassuring
when you're 38,000 feet up,
don't you think?

Underground Overheard Rambling Free

(a found poem)

If cheese had a penis, I'd marry it.
Do vegans eat meat?
It is a well known fact that vegans taste better.
Yes, I was sick in my Le Creuset dish.
I'm 95% single at the moment.
If I don't eat avocados, my breasts will get smaller.
I do like avocados, but that's not the reason
I can't afford to buy a house.
There's no comfortable place
for my tongue in my mouth.
It reminds me of the time I lit my shoe on fire
to heat a tin of ravioli in my dad's garage.
It had a pig-proof room.
That was before I was on hand gels.
Have you ever had a cold wee?
I once ate so much Monster Munch
my tongue began to bleed.
I wonder how many people would have to click together
to be heard in outer space.
What do you mean, "What are chickens supposed to do"?
This country is doomed – all we've got is badgers
and Theresa May. So drunk
that my phone didn't recognise my face.
Hungover is an emotion.
I bet Craig David goes quite well with ibuprofen.
He looks exactly like Shakespeare. Same beard, same haircut.
Lived his whole life without a spatula.
You have quinoa on your inner.
Do my fingers smell of fish?
Oh my God, I don't care.
Just pick an escalator.

A Capital Demand

Jobs in your area! Do YOU want to care?
We have vacancies everywhere, quality assured,
person-centred care and support.

Take your pick, we will fit you in. Fair pay,
hours that you want to work and holidays.
We're flexible, adaptable, you're able and available.

Great! And they've promised me
hours in my area. I won't have to travel too far.
Sign here ....

No you can't work there. Jobs in your area?
Don't you want to care?
We're a fair employer. 50p more
than the minimum wage.
Holidays?
Yes, they're unpaid.

You buy a bus pass.
Bus is delayed.
It only takes cash, doesn't take the pass,
and if you don't catch this, you'll be late.
So the price of the pass is a waste
and you won't get paid for the 45-minute-long wait.

Jobs in your area! Do YOU want to care?
We have vacancies everywhere.
Take Your Pick.
Not there.

Joe's safe's empty. Who's got the key?
Never mind that, rat-a-tat-tat, hurry up,
wake him up, make tea, change the bed,
then a 10-minute form-fill.
What happened to his other pills?
Get him into bed,
tucked up, 6pm.
A childhood bedtime for old grown men.
Don't worry. Just care.

Jobs in your area! Don't you want to work
for a minimum wage? Ungrateful.

Kate's in a rage.
A dozen eggs dashed on her kitchen floor,
one smashed teacup, the dog's gone spare,
blood *everywhere*
and a tiny time-slot to take care:

hoover mop brush clean calm cook dust hush the dog
and put a wash on.

Try to tempt Kate to eat tea.
Not hungry.
Leave her a butty that you know she won't eat.
Out the front door
for a 20-minute unpaid walk to the next.

It gets cancelled.
There's a 90-minute gap.
No point going home, costs too much.

So a 90-minute gap spent sat on a bench,
watching nothing but the time,

'cause at 9pm sharp you're off to Arthur's
to shower, shave, wipe his arse
and try to keep his dignity intact.

He never stops apologising all the way through,
his poor bent body doesn't work the way it used to.
He tells you all about it and your bus time comes

then goes,
'cause his list of reminiscences grows and grows.
He's not seen anybody all this week,
so when he starts to speak,
you haven't got the heart to leave him be
all alone, in his one-room,
four-wall cell of a home.

Jobs in your area! Don't you want to care?
We have vacancies everywhere.
You can't work there.
They died.

Ida needs an ambulance.
Not very well.
Blood sugar's loopy, feeling very funny.
Paramedics help, they treat her every Monday.
She's lucky this time, but your cortisol's high
and you're living on adrenaline again.

We'll send you a roster, text on a Sunday,
ring in your free time, stress guaranteed,
and if you don't speak now, you'll be in trouble.
Try to eke a living on a 6-hour week,
less bus fare.

Care and support.
Jobs in your area, quality assured.
Stop crying. Just care.
Wear a tiny little badge,
a gift from Matt,
with a capital demand
to
CARE.

Triptych

(after The Pillow Book *by Sei Shōnagon)*

Things That Make My Throat Close Over

The radio: Sibelius. Finlandia: the cello dread and brass intent
of poems written
afterwards, to tumble back before she left, for me
to hold the hand and turn the cogs
of my salty dog, bereft.
I cannot listen without echoes.

The unexpected note my lover leaves me on the table,
which I only see
when he is far away.

The Grapes of Wrath, especially the final paragraph.

Children being diminished, twisting into ruined seeds
in turn to reap rewards
of a festering sore. How no one seems to want to halt the entropy.

Babies made invisible, buried, hand-dug from hot rubble
and displayed to a weeping world. How rarely breaks the circle.

The Cliffs of Moher, where I became a stolen child, held breath,
and on my death
take my dust, dash me down. Let me join the drowned
and we'll roar
within Atlantic storms forever.

How Leonard Cohen wrote about his brother.

Things That Gnaw The Silence

That the fire in my belly grows cold. Anger's been an energy
since infancy.
It's impotent without the poisoned water.
When she left, gloves were down, seconds out, no more rounds,
the battle ended. Left empty on a ledge without a word
or deadly weapon,
looking down into the void.
I miss the venom. I understood the venom.

Things That Make A Difference To A Stranger

A smile given freely at the bus stop.

A chat about the rain, snow, sleet, wind, sunshine; daffodils, daisies,
how long lived, congratulations. Offering a helping hand with
bag, pram, jump leads.

Apologies. To take responsibility for wrongs that I committed
in the car park, motorway, one-way system.
Sorry, that was me.

Kindness. Simple acts of altruism, valueless and valuable,
the oil to the wheels of the world.
Cheery Hi's, Hello's and How's Your Days,
passing time, giving time
to those with the brittle flint of lonely in their eye.

How Leonard Cohen wrote about the cracks in everything.

i. *Viral Haiku*
ii. *Summer's Going Viral*
iii. *Salvation*
iv. *Streaming*
v. *?*
vi. *Operation Last Gasp*
vii. *The Ballad of Twat Mancock*
viii. *True Colours*
ix. *Moonshot Haiku*
x. *Impressions of a Curate's Egg*
xi. *Mixed Megassing*
xii. *Vision Haiku*
xiii. *Playing Bread*
xiv. *Long Division*
xv. *Blunt*
xvi. *Mutations*

Immorality
spread thick on supermarket
sandwiches. Eat shit.

Bulk-buying panic
bumps up the profit margin.
Retail rubs its hands.

Consideration
faked in multiple emails.
"We are sorry." Not.

Minimum wage slaves
battling bog roll abuse.
Frontline warriors.

Danger money now!
*Who'll defend the workers who
cannot organise?*

Summer's Going Viral

Summer's going viral.
We have new language.
Locked down, loaded up
with bog rolls, pasta,
bread and rice;
ice cream still available.

Summer's going viral.
The lingo's changing.
We're self-isolating,
t'internet's creaking,
working from home
is squeezing streaming.

Summer's going viral.
Lexicon's evolving.
Coughing is suspicious,
keep your social distance.
Ban mass gatherings.
Rationing's back.

Summer's going viral.
Stages empty, boots undanced,
we remain unenhanced,
unplugged, unhugged;
straight-edge hermits
with clean hands.

Summer's going viral.
Wakes unwoken, weddings
unattended, funerals empty.
All flights grounded.

Little solidarity in panicking
greed, ignoring poor and needy.

Summer's going viral.
We stay home, days unbrightened,
blue sky crisis. Balls unkicked,
goals unsaved, racing horses halted –
at least some of it's humane.

Summer's going viral.
Society spirals.
Hospitals inadequate. Doctors dying.
Tories forced to care
for the folk
they've despised so far.

We've all gone viral.
The most successful being
on the planet... is a pandemic.
We're doing more tests,
we're not quite sure if it's sentient
yet.

Salvation

We fucked in the morning,
before dawn's light
choked desire with uncertainty.
And the bees didn't know
and the birds didn't care
that economy's collapse
was hanging in the air,
but we were frozen.
Libidos crashed as society
smashed against the ground,
and just as the spring woke
land and lamb,
and bright sun rose
on magnolia's bloom,
butterfly's dusty rouse,
boom went bust,
jobs got lost,
futures broke
and national legs and lungs closed down.

We extracted empty promises
of ongoing hours
from bosses facing losses
on their capital gains.
Observed that poverty, profit and policy
never made love
though slept in the same wet bed.
But tenderness wrought
some comfort when
we fucked in the morning,
before dawn's light
choked desire with uncertainty.

With arms and legs wrapped tight
round love, we kissed the lips
of fear and fate,
made a nest
for us to hide
and hunker down
to safety.

The ice doesn't break
when glass and fibre cable come between us.

I don't know where to look.
There's no eye meeting mine;
no surprised eyebrows
shooting up in shock, fear,
click or commonality.

We try our best, but
the back room's lacking electricity.

I cannot cast my words
upon a sea of bobbing heads.
No sound coming back to me;
a blank of gasp and chuckle
or well-placed heckle.

I have no mic to push and pull,
to shake, or paint with venom.

All hollow, I echo, the acoustics
in this kitchen leave me wanting
engineers in a tent, field,
pub, back room or big marquee,
who know their shit.

And afterwards, the chasm
of no hands clapping.
No glass raised, back slapped,
handshake praise,
signed to a wife, mate,
mother or son.

Then where to put adrenaline?
Bring on 2021.

he's in good spirits
    sitting up in bed
        he's stable and engaging
            with the staff, being treated
            by the finest in the land
                he's opening his eyes
                    blinking yes or no
                        and he's doing just fine
                        getting better all the time
                        but there's no cheery selfie
                        and we don't see you
                        on the ICU Prime Minister
                        though we hear that you're
                        definitely *not* on a ventilator
                    still the boss of everyone
                a fighter, to be sure
              and you're improving
            proving to the whole wide world
            that you're responding to the treatment
          using subtle language
       to try and be discreet
     about how sick you really are
  so there's nowt to see
here folks, he's making
steady progress
please move
along because
he's

positively
absolutely
definitely
not on a
ventilator
is he?

Operation Last Gasp

He's being treated by the finest
and he'll waive those pesky visas
for at least another year
that would throw the finest medics
far away from here, and lock our doors
against their finest caring hands.
Please extend your stay, risk your very lives
for a government who'd have you play
at suicide in wards across this land
of hope and glory, decked out in fear
and worry, bunting made of PPE
viral papier-mâché.
Shake hands! Shake hands!
Where's your herd immunity?
I wonder if he understands his own advice
coughed him into hospital.
Operation Last Gasp not so funny now.

The Ballad of Twat Mancock

Every time I see his face, his sickly little grin,
I have an urge, it's building, and one day I'll give in.
It's for the best that I am never near the crusty sock,
or I would take him by the hair and back-hand Matt Hancock.

Yes, I would take a run up to that flannel of a man,
his soapy gob, all snooty strop, a walking pension plan.
Don't let me get in spitting distance; he will get a shock
when I grab his tiny bollocks and batter Matt Hancock.

His Tory titter, ceaseless smug, his twisted politics,
enrage me to a big red mist and fire up both my fists.
But I cannot and I will not go to prison for the cock,
so won't take him by the ankles and twat that Matt Hancock.
No, I'm not doing time, so I won't smash up Matt Hancock,
and I will keep my liberty and not whack Matt Hancock.

You say you are a Socialist.
You do not trust the government.
You share misinformation,
Fuck their rules and regulations.

You do not want to wear a mask,
will not be 'muzzled', can't be arsed.
You care about your fellow man,
but shun collective safety.

You don't believe the mainstream news.
Your 'research' comes from echoed views
on YouTube, Q and obscure sites,
not scientific evidence.

You share a shoulder, wide and warm,
but won't be told, will not 'conform'.
You risk the health of everyone,
refer to us as sheeple.

I love you, but I don't believe
you see a Truth that I can't see.
Your song is from the other side,
your left wing's formed a red right hand.

Community contains a power.
We overcome our darkest hours.
We help ourselves collectively,
in altruistic harmony.

It isn't Left, it isn't right
to spit on comrades from great heights.

Your dog whistle politics
are pissing down my leg.

You say you are a Socialist.
I see an individualist
dispensing with the medicine
that lets our people breathe.

Moonshot Haiku

Moonshot ambition;
bukkake for the nation.
Pass the flannel, please.

Impressions of a Curate's Egg

It was the best of times,
it was the worst of times.
It didn't miss a trick
of the spring bells
and yellows, daffodil's bloom.
Sitting in the long grass
on golden afternoons
hearing nothing, no brawls,
no Friday siren calls.
Mean streets bleached
with a bucketful of shut pubs,
rubbish unstrewn, unspewed-on pavements.
Sky blind blue, buzzard-full,
close focus of our 20/20 vision.
Trade not exhaling desire.

It was smiles wide as wasteland
walked on our doorstep,
deeper to explore every pocket,
nature's locker for an office.
Rare ponds, bramble-racked,
mapped for the autumn.
It wasn't packed motorways,
bus, train, traffic jams,
nose-to-tail delays or verbal warnings.

It was Protecting Our NHS,
empty shelf selfishness,
staying home, injecting disinfectant.
Untested elderly, triaged in reverse,
DNR'd without regard,
dispensing with disposable community.

It wasn't herd immunity
even though Pat Vallance said it was,
on the telly.
Galloping mortality, soap-sud slides.
Just in from Durham, Pinocchio advised
that his tongue was as long as a telephone wire.
Bridges burning, lesson learning, medics muted
by a minister primed to divide
and conquer truth.

It was paper rainbows, Thursday claps,
pots and pans banged
for the badge
that Matt had offered,
not the pay rise, that he didn't.
It was Cheltenham, Atletico, "official advice".
It wasn't quarantining incoming flights.
A week too late for 20,000 graves,
grief borne alone in isolation.

It was One. Bin. Bag. One. Glove. Then. Another.
60,000 deaths on an island with the borders
that you fought on
and failed to control.
Three-word slogans
that didn't make the grade.
It's still no vaccination,
infection rising daily.
It had listened to the science,
but now it's back to work,
school, tube-bred winter of our discontent
and ravaged population.

Barthes, Saussure and Derrida walk into a bar.
Barthes sports a Batman mask, nestled beneath his nose.
Saussure wears a visor, a surgical mask, pinny and gloves.
Derrida questions the premise of protection,
cuts an iron mask to rags with a blunt razor blade.
"It's 10pm," says the landlord, tapping his watch. "Get out."
Barthes dismisses this information,
repeatedly beating the landlord
over the head with the world's clock.
Saussure repeats
the landlord's speech,
finishing the sentence with an upward inflection?
Derrida speaks for over an hour
on the subject of clowns in power and the
performative arts,
emphases in strange places.
They fail to play darts;
no agreement can be reached on the rules.
They appear on the telly the very next day
in place of Charlie Cairoli, JVT and Tintin.
Well if a job's worth doing, it's worth doing well.

Vision Haiku

We see clearly now.
The year of perfect vision
blinded by bombast.

Clowns in high places
juggled monkeys flinging shit.
Double-tongued circus.

Critical moment.
New measures. Tackling. Rules
changing. Viable?

They have lost control.
We never really had it.
Broken rhetoric.

500g wholemeal flour
1
100
2 tsp dried yeast
2
3, 000
Salt milk honey butter
38, 000
Water, seeds
43
Oil for greasing
60
Combine
to 70, 80 plus
Bring milk to the boil in
90, 000
Remove from heat, gradually add
One Hundred and Seventeen Thousand
Knead and prove
Brazilian, Kent
Sprinkle seeds
New variant
Brush and bake
South Africa
Stay at home in a

    lemon drizzle, cupcake, banana bread limbo.
    Jam tart, crumble, sourdough daze.
    Need and feed and break 'til hollow.
    We play bread in a lockdown glaze.

This is a divisive poem.
It gags at jabs, refuses 'muzzles',
condescends to old friends, alienates the new.
Hates. Bill. Gates.
Says "real eyes realize the real lies".
Denies we're all in danger from the plague.
Uses YouTube in debates on social media
(without shame),
then rages, rants, defriends and makes
the world a sicker place.

This is a divisive poem.
It twitches curtains, judges neighbours,
tuts at strangers in the park, joggers puffing germs,
and wears a worried frown in the Asda.
It's consumed by bending rules,
will outline them for you
if you have an hour or two to spare,
2 metres distant, of course.
It will give you chapter, book and verse,
and all the world's statistics.
It knows the definition of a bubble.

This is a divisive poem.
Ignores all warnings, New World Order
rules and regulations,
thinks *everything* is fake
and paints itself into a corner.
Disregards evidence from independent bodies,
(apart from David Icke),
sees conspiracy in every conversation.
It will not be silenced by the deep sheep state.
Baaa.

This poem has not lost control
nor has it been buffoonish
in the hope of shaking blame
from its scruffy blond mane.
It didn't wait months to test incoming flights,
make monumental cock-ups,
pay consultants top dollar on a
project that has failed to deliver.
It hasn't banged lecterns, burbling lectures
that its friends will just ignore and get away with.
Alas!
Did not protect the NHS, save lives or stay at home.

This is a divisive poem.
It's up against a wall, shot full of bullets
made of ridicule and misplaced rebellion.
It cannot be performed, half the audience
will hate it, the other half will heckle,
and no one wants to hear about pandemics anymore.
It does not want to talk about
the year of perfect vision,
my position, yours.
It would rather have a hug,
chat shit, pass the rum.
It would rather leave division far behind.
It would rather you remember
where the real blame lies
when it's time to kiss the ballot box again.

Blunt

Like a 2B pencil
with no cutting edge available;
lines faint to grey,
definition bleeds away.

Like a razor blade left
on a bathroom shelf
forgets precision,
the harmony of rhythm.

Like a mitten, glove, fuzzy
felt farm scene, nuzzling
pre-cut pretend play
day-to-day activities.

Faculties
lost in the feathers
of a pillow fight, empty
non-entities, dulled-down memories.

A dart
without flight, falling far
from the bull, double top,
nil point; clock stopped.

Like a knife
without steel, stone, fight,
or a ham to hold purpose
in a lifelike pose.

Like a small axe
robbed of its big tree reason,
we are dull; blunt to weather
wood's depletion.

We would like a happy ending here.
We *would* like a happy ending here.
We would *like* a happy ending here.
We would like a *happy* ending here.
We would like a happy *ending* here.
We would like an ending.

HERE.

On Sliabh Mis mountain, Foley's Glen,
the Widow Scotia lies in wait.
Incantations meld with mist
and twist in curl and bloom of cloud,
avowed to wreak revenge
on Celtic kings.

Four hundred years before Our Lord,
belly-heavy, battle-torn,
the Pharaoh's daughter drew her sword
for to avenge her husband dear.
Her stumble-steed, in error, fell,
and now she bides in Foley's Glen.

And how she keens, how she moans,
the Widow Scotia, Pharaoh's daughter;
all these years of grief and tears,
all this time alone.

Carving wrath in silt and stone,
she cuts her tongue on jagged banks.
Only Sister Silver sees
the green she spits upon the rocks
for wanderers to skid and crump
and feed her fierce hunger.

With ancient tongue, and hate within,
she conjures sinew, muscle, skin.
She seeks Dé Danann – *stand aside!*
She'll jump upon your back astride
and with an awful curdle-cry,
she'll ride your flesh to bone.

And how she bellows! How she crows!
The Widow Scotia, Pharaoh's daughter;
all these years of bitter sorrow
feast upon today.

To those who deem her cruel and cold,
a spectral terror, heinous crone:
this desolate and broken soul
has lost her lover, children, home.
Cast not your one-eyed pious stone.
She's trapped in Foley's Glen,
alone forever.

Mighty is the gull whose head I slept in,
who lent me feathers for seconds
or hours, allowed her eyes
to show me shining waters;
skimmed an inch above the surf,
cyclical in air,
in thermal lift.

Eternal thanks
for taking hold of human hands,
filling them with sky and sea,
teaching them to fly.
They have longed to learn such simple tricks.
I have no gift to match this.
Cannot show you how we rush
like water on the wind,
or salt your tongue and teeth,
rippling each hollow shaft;
every waft a warping curve,
brushing heaven's hair.

To pour this liquid into skin,
strip your flight of fancy,
feel our dreadful burden
or the ache of human gravity
on clumsy clatterbones
would wound us both.
For your balm to soothe the sadness
and cleanse my day of strain,
I hold your essence in my fingertips,
pray for safe sojourn
and liberty that lasts
an ocean's span.

Long he lay and looked and loved
his own sweet face,
his own sweet face.
Long he lay and looked.

Himself an echo, manifest.
He was possessed.
He was possessed.
He had no other thought.

He wanted water on his lips
to kiss complete,
to kiss complete;
to penetrate, possess.

He cupped the beauty in the pool.
Drank him down, long and cool.
Drank him down, long and cool,
diminishing the youth.

He lay and looked and longed for love.
His thirst now unrequited.
His thirst now unrequited.
His heart began to break.

Consumed, he lost the will to live.
Love annulled with every sip.
Love annulled with every sip.
He drank himself to death.

Manspreader

Hey Billy Big Balls,
spreading on the seat,
just how much space does one man need?
Did you buy two tickets,
one for each knee?
'Cause they're taking up the space that *my* legs need.

Hey Billy Big Balls,
spreading on the train,
such a vast sack must cause you pain.
Have you been to the doctor,
or had them examined?
'Cause they shouldn't be the size of a cantaloupe melon.

Hey Billy Big Balls,
spreading on the tube,
your tittylip's out when I ask you to move.
Do they need to be aired?
Are you about to give birth?
Were you born a selfish cunt or did you have to learn?

Hey Billy Big Balls,
spreading on the bus,
sitting like your genitals are all puffed up.
Are your undies like a hammock
to accommodate your knackers?
It's a wonder you can even stand up.

Hey Billy Big Balls,
spreading everywhere,
when I do it to you back, are your feelings hurt?

Is your ego squashed?
Will it ruin your cock?
How does it feel when I take space up?

Hey Billy Big Balls,
arrogant twat,
you get the width of your seat,
no more than that.
Can you shut your knees please?
Can you not sulk
when I politely ask you
"Are you the fucking Hulk?
Are you a Superhero?
Are your goolies monumental?
Is your scrotum fucking epic?
Or are you just a massive prick?"

Bank Robber (Me Granny Was)

Me granny was a bank robber.
She never hurt nobody.
But no one could describe her face
so she's immensely wealthy.

Some is young, some is old,
and that's the way the world is,
but I don't believe in moaning on
about your many wrinkles.

Barclays have CCTV.
They might as well not bother,
'cause gran is at that certain age
where no one ever sees her.

So she came to rob NatWest,
the TSB and Santander.
Break your nails to earn your pay.
Don't need no balaclava.

Me granny was a bank robber.
She never hurt nobody.
But no one could describe her face
so she's immensely wealthy.

The perfect age for a life of crime
begins when you turn 59.
Witnesses will only see
your grey hair and an outline.

Bystanders will testify
"I think she had a zimmer.

A rainmac, was it blue or grey?
I really can't remember."

Someday you'll meet your rocking chair,
brittle bones, dementia.
Until that day, gran, get your gun,
appropriate some moolah.

Me granny was a bank robber.
She never hurt nobody.
But no one could describe her face
so she's immensely wealthy.

Get away, get away, get away, get away, get away, get away, get away.

Run granny run!

With Reasonable Force

Spare the rod and spoil the child!
Never did me no harm.
It's what we called a *good hiding*.
How else are they gonna learn?
You'll feel the back of my hand, young man,
I'll box your ears for sure.
I reserve the right to use reasonable force
to physically punish the small.

I refuse to see the irony,
recycling of fury,
desensitizing little kids,
stamping on their dignity.
My hypocrisy, it knows no bounds,
I'll teach them not to bully!
I reserve the right to use reasonable force
to establish infant boundaries.

It's not confusing double standards,
this is my Authority!
They'll do just what I bloody say,
not what I bloody do, okay?
I wouldn't do this to an adult,
it's a punishable crime!
But I reserve the right to use reasonable force,
inflict it on my child.

Slipper, cane, knuckle, fist,
instil mistrust and bitterness.
Paddle, hairbrush, leather strap,
build resentment, slap by slap.

Father's belt, mother's palm
calmly doles out injury.
They reserve the right to use reasonable force
on their own defenceless progeny.

It takes too long to talk about
the ways to deal with life.
It's too much trouble chatting to
this human being of mine.
I haven't got the patience
to explain the wrong from right,
so instead I'll take the easy route
and smack into compliance.
It's not assault, it's justified,
within the bounds of duty.
I reserve the right to use reasonable force,
treat violence with barbarity.

That'll learn 'em!

Fur coat, no knickers.
No better than she ought to be.
Common as muck.
Too clever for her own good.

Slung out lines to stunt and mould,
ensure she doesn't reach her goals.
Keep her tight inside a box,
locked away from greatness.

Slappers, tarts, MILFs and cougars,
girl next door with Page 3 hooters,
sluts and slags and dirty bitches,
fried egg tits and split-arse wenches.

Acronyms and words to wound,
imbued with hatred, ugly tools
of fucked up fools and bully boys
unable to enjoy a woman's company.

'er indoors, the wife, the slice,
she's ruined now she's had a child.
Throw one up her, fuck her blind;
a sausage up an alleyway.

Shaped and shorn from puberty,
language used to keep us meek.
We live and breathe the daily stench
of all the world's misogyny.

To all the boys, big and small,
here's a little helper:
never call a woman
what you wouldn't call your daughter.

Invasive

If I possessed a phone back then,
would it help or hinder?
They're calling it *disclosure*.
Those men were ten years older.
They said it was a party,
I believed them.
Would the phone show "asking for it",
"look at what she did and said,
dirty girls deserve to learn a lesson"?

If I had owned a mobile phone,
would it show Authority that teenage promiscuity
is often born of need?
Of hunger for affection,
love in any currency?
A fight against morality?
And if it did, would it say
my body is my business, not to be dismissed
and narrowed down, opened up,
one unbroken flow of always yes and never no?

Would the bottle of Bacardi that they gave me
be on Instagram?
Evidence of ever more debauchery?
Perhaps there would be photos of me
sprawled across the bed, dead drunk,
limbs numb, and unable to co-ordinate defence.
Perhaps there would be videos,
diminishing *No*'s
and the noises men make.
Maybe not.

Distance doesn't medicate
or mediate the damage done;
tranquillity's impossible for some,
full disclosure.
I'm over thirty years older.
They said it was a party.
But it wasn't.

If it was your son,
you'd want to know why,
wouldn't you?
What was on his mind?
Could it be predicted?
If he became the source of a statistic often quoted,
of a crime doubled up, year upon year,
I think you'd want to know.
Or would you veer away?
Never ask yourself why
he reacted in that way.
Did you raise your voice too often
in his formative years,
or not enough?

> And everybody said
> *He just wasn't like that.*

> And everybody said
> *Such a lovely man.*

So what about role models, what about culture,
what about assumptions of a patriarchal nature?
You're pretty sure he never saw
that kind of thing from you, but
was he mummy's little soldier?
Daddy's brave boy?
Was he strong, did he dominate,
hide himself away behind a big brick wall
that he built with his terrified fists?

> And everybody said
> *He didn't have it in him.*

And everybody said
Devoted to his wife.

He's a surgeon, soldier, salesman, cabbie,
policeman, postman, fireman, brickie;
husband, father, pillar of society.
The pride of the provider,
entitled to his property.
At what point did he crack?
Didn't want to hand them back,
because if he can't have them, no one else can.
It's the last big thing that daddy can do
now that mummy doesn't love him anymore.

So he drives to the river,
or the edge of a cliff,
takes a big pillow,
a knife or some pills,
gives the kids lollies,
leaves a bitter note,
and they will never go home
and they will never grow old
and they will never have kids of their own.

And everybody said
I can't believe he did it.

And everybody said
Such a great dad.

And his wife and his kids say
nothing, 'cause they can't.

So what of frogs, what of snails,
what of puppy-dog tails?
Expendable offspring, pawns in a game?

What of ordinary men, extraordinary acts,
toxic masculinity, leader of the pack?
What of horror and abhorrence,
jealousy, possession?

And how do we ensure
that the next generation
doesn't generate more of the same?

Mavis had a room
that didn't have a name.

You did not dine.
You did not live.
It was not kitchen.
Was not front.
Was not back or parlour.

Mavis had this furniture
that I had never seen.

It was not settee.
Was not armchair.
Was not pouffe,
for phone,
or couch divan.

Mavis had this massive room
full of fiery light.

Floaty motes looped in rays
like lasers onto *French windows*
that looked out on her *pa-tee-oh*
where goldfish bobbed and bubbled
all around a cooling pool.

Mavis had a *broh-cade* stool,
no arms or back to it.

Broad and cushioned lushful seating,
made to sit and play the thing
it sat so grand in front of –

majestically ivoried,
two-tone keys to soothe.

I remember wanting Mavis
to be my real mum

so I could sit in sunshine
playing music to myself
in her beautifully useless room without a name;
to sit on stones and tickle fish
in safe and silent solitude
for more than just
one golden afternoon.

To have grown without the grain of hate,
to sleep and want to wake before the school day starts.
To finally believe in happy endings, and beginnings,
and later, to know that it wasn't my fault.
To not be the crop she raised from kernel
to a raging field of fire, taking
half a span and passing to extinguish.
To not walk wanting, or wounded through the stubble,
smoke lying low on the horizon,
watching spiral wisps of what could be
and wasn't.

To be raised in a meadow full of buttercups and trust,
and a smile sweetly meant, malice furthest
from the heart as other galaxies to Earth.
To not look for love
in all the thorny places,
from other damaged crops,
recreating origins.
To know enough to realise
that kindness rears the highest yield,
the taller trees, unbent.

What I didn't have myself
I made a present of,
unwrapped and unconditional.
Swaddled her in safe
to grow as tall as trees are meant to grow,
knowing that my heart is hers,
that I am always there in a meadow
full of buttercups and trust.

Beatitude

We may not light so many fires,
but I'll be yours if you'll be mine.
Shallow eyes see lines and grooves,
but I see wise and warm and weft,
there's plenty left.
I see proof of life.

Four score and twenty lie between
our bellies, bigger than before,
but soft and more for us to hold.
We fold together, tender
in our wrinkled sheets,
and I can see it in your eyes;
we may not light so many fires,
but I am yours and you are mine.

We are not bound by gold or ink,
but when one sinks, the other lifts,
no one drowns,
and when the darkness comes within,
whisper circles on my skin,
let me see how to begin again.

Love is not a cul-de-sac
or paper stained with certainty,
duty-bound or locked in obligation,
but an avenue, a motorway,
an endless path meandering,
holding hands until we reach
our final destination.

Though we sometimes fall and falter,
lose our grip in helter-skelter,
human flaws making diamonds
fall from both our eyes,
salt and glitter, just remember
I am yours and you are mine
and we're alive together,
lighting fires at twilight.

Friendship Haiku

So some are for spring,
all grin and beginning to
blossom in summer;

some are for summer.
Starlight delighting, whisky
and 6am chat;

some are for autumn,
dancing with gold in our grey.
Halfway to darkness;

some are for winter.
Skin withers slack, we loiter
and hope to make spring;

some are for ever,
weathered by grief, leaving us
lost in your silence.

We'll be okay, we've got plenty of experience.
You can be a cabbie, I'm sure you can handle
cleaning vomit off upholstery,
lairy lads on Friday night, gobby girls smoking in the back.
We don't need their help Harry, bollocks to your nan.
You can learn the lingo, I can teach you Cockerney.
We don't need their money after all.
We'll manage, our marriage will be stronger when we're poor.

I'll return to acting, or *Celebrity Whatever*,
Big Brother, *Strictly*, *The Voice*, the list is endless,
we'll be reet. Did you hear me Harry? *"We'll be reet."*
Perhaps I'll get a role on *Coronation Street*.
I've clearly mastered dialect.
We don't need their privilege.
We'll manage, our marriage will be stronger when we're skint.

I could be a Dinner Lady, dishing up 'spuds'.
I'd look pretty good in a tabard, don't you think?
Gingham really suits me.
You could do sales, I can see you in a suit.
Your la-di-da accent would go down a real treat.
Beemers only, of course, or maybe Rovers, Landies,
like your grandad liked to crash on the estate.
We'll be fine, we'll manage, our marriage will be stronger
when we're skint.

I could deal down the park. I'm sharky
when I want to be. I'll undercut the youth,
all louche, underclass, keep a blade in my bag,
offer top-class buds, bit of pollen, Moroccan,
balloons for the loons, 50p a go.

Or there's Tesco, Aldi, as long as we agree
to work 24/7/365, we'll be fine.
Our marriage will be stronger on the breadline.

You could wash cars at the garage of a Sunday.
I might fancy you more, bit of rough with your chamois.
And if we're really poor, we could even draw 'dole'
or whatever it's called.
Free money, my love, no different than before!
We'll be fine, we'll manage, we can't afford a carriage,
but our marriage will be stronger when we're poor,
I'm sure.
Common people do it, after all.

i. Fishy

After the first frost,
orange ice cubes decorate
our Japanese pond.

ii. Secret

I never told her
what I did to her pet dog
when she wasn't there.

some people feel the rain, others get
rode hard and put away
behind the ears
the baby's head
a hen, your feet
a line
a weekend

but not quite an appetite
beak stone or whistle

it is not itself

Three days later,
we bought a Newton's cradle.
Put it on the table, and heartsick,
tried to *click click click* our way out of it.
But there's six strings missing,
a great big grin,
and a legendary faux fur coat.

There are two types of energy:
potential and *kinetic.*
One is energetic, inhabiting space.
One anticipates
velocity, force.
It cannot be destroyed.
Waits in the wings,
electricity intact,
and it lives when we sing and remember.

Three days later,
we bought a Newton's cradle.
Put it on the table, and heartsick,
tried to *click click click* our way out of it.
Then collision click clacked, slowed to a tick,
to a whisper, to collective,
from kinetic to potential.

It's said that friction robs the system of its energy,
but really, the universe desires to commune.

'Plump' – the collective noun for a group of geese on the ground is a gaggle; when in flight, they are called a skein, a team, or a wedge; when flying close together, they are called a plump.

'The Last Shanty' documents my dad's Royal Navy Committal in Portsmouth.

'Underground Overheard Rambling Free' is a found poem. Sources were originally from the London Underground, which were then printed in *Time Out*, and repeated on Twitter.

'World-Beating Corona Suite' – Boris Johnson used the phrase 'world-beating' in relation to the Test and Trace system, the contract for which was handed to Baroness and Conservative life peer Dido Harding (at an eye-watering cost of £37 billion over 2 years, plus £1000 to £6000 a day consultancy fees), and which turned out to be anything but world-beating. The poems in this section run in the order they were written, from the first lockdown to the last.

'Viral Haiku' is from a Billy Bragg lyric, "There is Power in a Union".

'Streaming' – when all gigs got cancelled, artists began to 'live stream' from their homes. I can't begin to tell you how strange it is to perform to a webcam in a silent empty room. The last line may prove to be somewhat optimistic.

'?' – Boris Johnson was rushed to intensive care in hospital after collapsing with Covid-19, a couple of weeks after boasting about shaking hands with Covid patients in hospital.

'Operation Last Gasp' – Boris Johnson was hospitalised with Covid-19 soon after joking that the emergency project to build more life-saving ventilators could be known as 'Operation Last Gasp'.

'Moonshot haiku' is inspired by Boris Johnson's 'moonshot' plan to roll out a Covid-19 saliva test (which didn't exist at the time) to every person in the UK, at a time when testing capacity was falling far short of meeting demand.

'Impressions of a Curate's Egg' – a Curate's Egg is something that is partly bad and partly good, but mostly bad. 60,000 deaths refers to excess mortality (above the average expected for the time of year). At least one order of PPE was counted individually, so one glove, then another, etc. In this way, the Govt could say they had supplied a million items. Durham is where Dominic Cummings drove to whilst his wife was ill with Covid, and he was infected with it, when the country was locked down. He also drove 30 minutes to Barnard Castle, apparently to test his eyesight. The "badge that Matt had offered" relates to Matt Hancock recognising the bravery and hard work of homecare workers not with a decent wage or better working conditions, but rather with a green badge that said CARE.

'Mixed Megassing' references several semioticians, and refers to the constant mixed messages given out by the Govt. JVT is Jonathan Van Tam and Tintin refers to Chris Witty, both regulars on the Covid press briefings. Charlie Brooker hilariously described the latter as "A sad Doctor resembling Tintin prematurely aged after watching his dog drown". Charlie Cairoli was a famous clown.

'Playing Bread' – when the new variants became apparent in their rapidly-increasing mortality rates, Lockdown 3 was put in place. The nation baked as the death rate more than doubled.

'Long Division' – uses a lot of the Covid lexicon. Qanon conspiracy theorists, anti-vaxxers and virus-deniers believed the pandemic was a cover for a plan to implant trackable microchips in the vaccine, and that Bill Gates was behind it. Yes, really. A 'bubble' was an allowable combination of people who could get together for various reasons (support, childcare). There was much talk of a New World Order and the Deep State (the latter very vocally publicised by ex-President Donald Trump, he of injecting disinfectant fame). Boris Johnson was fond of banging lecterns and barking "Alas" for effect. Friendships were broken, lost, and remain to be mended over the whole debacle.

'Blunt' – to get through over a year of lockdowns with loss of all freedoms, gigs, festies, family and friends, we had to blunt our emotions. I wonder if we'll ever fully recover.

'Mutations' – just as we thought there was light at the end of the tunnel, the Indian variant – now known as the Delta variant – made a last dash and started to become the main viral threat.

'Once Upon A Time' is based on the Irish myth of Queen Scotia.

'Bank Robber' is with deepest apologies to Joe Strummer and Mick Jones. I was trying to find the positives in becoming old and apparently 'invisible'. Sorry fellas.

'With Reasonable Force' – when Scotland announced a ban on smacking children in 2017, the uproar from adults intent on committing violence on children was both predictable and depressing. Parents still have a legal right to smack children in England, if they "only" use "reasonable force".

'Invasive' refers to the "digital strip search" disclosure requests that rape victims are subject to during legal investigations. The CPS denies that mobile phone data is used to cast doubt on the credibility of complainants, and that there is an increase in "No Further Action" being applied to cases where no consent is given.

'Frogs and Snails' is about the ever-growing prevalence of 'family annihilators'. See Prof. David Wilson's study at bcu.ac.uk/news-events/news/characteristics-of-family-killers-revealed-by-first-classification-study.

'Stronger When We're Poor' is my take on when Prince Harry and Megan Markle decided they were going to 'go it alone', without the help of the Royal Family.

'wet' – being a liquid, water is not itself wet, but can make other solid materials wet. Wetness is the ability of a liquid to adhere to the surface of a solid, so when we say that something is wet, we mean that the liquid is sticking to the surface of a material. Mind blown.

'Orisin' is an archaic word for prayer. This poem is for Boo Long, who left behind a Boo-shaped hole in everyone who had the privilege of knowing him.

'Speaking in Tongues' was previously published in *Release a Rage of Red*, the Bread and Roses Poetry Award Anthology 2019.

'Untangle' was shortlisted in the Wolverhampton Literature Festival Poetry Competition 2019, and published in their anthology.

'In Plain Sight' was shortlisted in the Wolverhampton Literature Festival Poetry Competition 2020, and published in their anthology

'Plump' was previously published in *Release a Rage of Red*, the Bread and Roses Poetry Award Anthology 2019 (under the incorrect name of J Holt Wilson!). The last line is taken from Gerard Winstanley's *The True Levellers' Standard Advanced* aka *The First Digger Manifesto* (1649).

'Recipe for Change' was published in the autumn 2019 'Crone Power' edition of *Gyroscope Review*.

A version of 'Underground Overheard Rambling Free' was published in *Overheard*, the Live from Worktown Anthology 2019.

'Viral Haiku' & 'Summer's Going Viral' both first appeared in Roundhead Publications' 2020 anthology *Coronaverses: Poems from the Pandemic*.

'Salvation' was a winner in the Bread and Roses Poetry Award 2020 and published in their anthology *Handbook for 2021*.

'Frogs and Snails' was published in *Citizen32*'s 2019 'Resistance and Revolution' edition.

'Unconditional' was first published in *Persephone's Daughters, Vol. 6*.

'Beatitude' was first published in autumn 2019's edition of *Printed Words*.

'wet' was published in Highland Park Poetry's autumn 2019/ winter 2020 'Muses Gallery'.

'Orison' was published in *Griffith Review #66: The Light Ascending*.

"Speaking in tongues indeed! Tongues of fire in a time of plague. Raging against conspiracy theorists, defending the vulnerable, the homeless, the old, the hardest hit in the worst of times. Words for the stage and words for the page from a supremely clever working-class poet who has quite literally been there, done it and got the T-shirt. It's one of mine, and bears the Adrian Mitchell quote which inspires poets who seek to connect: "Most people ignore most poetry because most poetry ignores most people." Another great collection."

— *Attila the Stockbroker, poet & musician*

"Laura Taylor is a natural ranter and tremendous performer of her work. Her energy, anger and passion are apparent in every word and gesture. And yes, in this collection there are examples of the fury we might expect from Taylor, and fans of her stage appearances will not be disappointed. It is a collection worth the cover price for 'The Ties That Bind' alone, which is a masterclass in her brand of well-executed poetry that hits home and hits hard (a poem which probably should be heard by everyone, and anthologised everywhere). Yet *Speaking in Tongues* offers so much more than excellent ranting. The central section, 'World-Beating Corona Suite' gives us incisive pieces about the UK's handling of the global pandemic, and is a poetic record of things which should not be forgotten. Elsewhere, we are treated to quiet observations and flights of fancy including 'In the mirror is an ocean', which starts with a magical "Mighty is the gull whose head I slept in,/who lent me feathers for seconds". There is too, biting satire as realised in 'Stronger When We're Poor'. And there are the beautiful lyrical pieces such as 'Login*' and the heartbreaking 'Mavis'. For me this is a must-have collection. This is Taylor at her best. She is well-read and eloquent (even when in full-on rant mode this is evident). Her writing is urgent, powerful and her punches land. Go see her perform. Buy this book."

— *Emma Purshouse, poet laureate for Wolverhampton*

"If there were an equivalent of *Masterchef* for cooking words into exquisitely tasty and surprising dishes, then Laura Taylor would win it. Whether she is holding forth on the menopause, working at sea, migration, or strange things said by fellow passengers, she takes raw words, mixes and simmers them, adds spices and a sprinkle of humour, and serves up course after course of thought-provoking dishes. Hot. Flavourful. Authentic. Instant pleasure with a long, lingering aftertaste."

— *Janine Booth, poet & writer*

"Those familiar with Taylor's on-stage persona will enjoy this distillation of her new work onto the page. *Speaking in Tongues* is at times forceful and at others lyrical as the author dances between haiku and concrete poetry, crosses from personal to political and cross-examines who we were and who we have become."

— *Winston Plowes, poet*

"These are poems to have a beer with, poems to sit round a fire and keep warm with, poems to rage against the system with, poems to take to the streets with. An extraordinary collection for extraordinary times."

— *Steph Pike, poet*

"This is Taylor's best yet. Her language is lush and confident, and her range is limitless. Whether "exorcising scribbles made of air and formless urges" (isn't that perfect?) or startling the reader with "Mighty is the gull whose head I slept in", by way of polemic such as 'The Ties that Bind' or the heartbreaking 'Invasive', or the Covid-themed 'Impressions of a Curate's Egg' that captures the Zeitgeist: Taylor's poetry is wise, honest, funny, angry, mature and assured. "Love is not a cul-de-sac/or paper stained with certainty", but this book is the tonic we all need."

— *Cathy Thomas-Bryant, poet & writer*